LIZARDS
AS A NEW PET
JOHN COBORN

CONTENTS

Distributed in the UNITED STATES by T.F.H. Publications, Inc., One T.F.H. Plaza, Neptune City, NJ 07753; in CANADA to the Pet Trade by H & L Pet Supplies Inc., 27 Kingston Crescent, Kitchener, Ontario N2B 2T6; Rolf C. Hagen Ltd., 3225 Sartelon Street, Montreal 382 Quebec; in CANADA to the Book Trade by Macmillan of Canada (A Division of Canada Publishing Corporation), 164 Commander Boulevard, Agincourt, Ontario M1S 3C7; in ENGLAND by T.F.H. Publications, PO Box 15, Waterlooville PO7 6BQ; in AUSTRALIA AND THE SOUTH PACIFIC by T.F.H. (Australia) Pty. Ltd., Box 149, Brookvale 2100 N.S.W., Australia; in NEW ZEALAND by Ross Haines & Son, Ltd., 82 D Elizabeth Knox Place, Panmure, Auckland, New Zealand; in the PHILIPPINES by Bio-Research, 5 Lippay Street, San Lorenzo Village, Makati, Rizal; in SOUTH AFRICA by Multipet Pty. Ltd., P.O. Box 35347, Northway, 4065, South Africa. Published by T.F.H. Publications, Inc. Manufactured in the United States of America by T.F.H. Publications, Inc.

Classification of the Lizards

Two hundred fifty years ago, man's knowledge of zoology was sparse and confusing. Although many animals had common names, these names differed from language to language and even from dialect to dialect. In addition, animals had not been studied in depth, and the different groups were not adequately distinguished from each other. For example, all amphibians were included with the reptiles; a lizard was a lizard, but a newt was a water lizard. We now know just how different these groups really are.

The science of identifying and giving names to animal (and plant) species is known as taxonomy; and the first taxonomist to devise a workable and practical system of classification was a Swedish botanist by the name of Karl von Linne (1707-1788). Linne, or Linnaeus as he preferred to call himself, took on the mammoth task of naming all the then known species of plant and animal under a system of binomial nomenclature. Under this system, each species is given two Latin (or Latinized) names. The first name is the *generic* name, the second is the *specific* name. The generic name is the name of the genus, a group (usually) of closely related species, while the specific name identifies the species within the genus.

Providing a species with its two names is not without problems, however, and in some cases it is necessary to add a third name, making a trinomial. This is used when geographical groups of certain species show certain differences, but are not sufficiently different to be considered as separate species. Such groups of animals are known as *subspecies*. While many lizards are regarded just as species, with a binomial, some may have quite a large number of subspecies.

Housing

There are no hard and fast rules regarding the type of housing required for captive lizards, but there are some general requirements that must be considered before obtaining any specimens. A cage in which lizards are kept may be called a vivarium or a terrarium (I prefer the latter name). A terrarium must be escape-proof, it must be of sufficient size for the animals being kept, and it must be supplied with the necessary life-support systems required by the species (heating, lighting, humidity, ventilation, etc.). Additionally, it should be easy to clean and service and should have an esthetically pleasing appearance.

Terrarium shapes are unimportant, providing the parameters mentioned above are taken into consideration. However, it is wise to use fairly tall terraria for arboreal (climbing or tree-dwelling) species and relatively shallow ones for terrestrial (ground-dwelling) types. It is now possible to buy commercial terraria in fiberglass or metal, complete with all needed life-support systems, but many enthusiasts still prefer to make their own. They may be constructed from various materials or modified from commercially purchased tanks of various types.

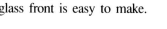

WOODEN TERRARIA

Wood can be used to construct a terrarium for animals to be kept at a low humidity, but it is not suitable for use in permanently damp conditions as, even with a few coats of varnish, it will quickly deteriorate. A simple terrarium consisting of a plywood box with a framed glass front is easy to make.

A basic terrarium that will successfully hold a small lizard for a few weeks until a better cage is available. The top should be anchored more securely. Photo: E. Radford.

3

Using half-inch marine or outdoor plywood, the top, bottom, back, and ends are cut to size and either securely glued and nailed together or fastened to a simple frame. The glass viewing panel may be slid into grooves on the top and bottom or in the sides, or you may wish to mount the glass in a wooden frame that can be hinged onto the box.

Groups of ventilation holes should be drilled in the ends of the cage about a third the distance up from the base to the top, and further holes should be drilled in the top to allow for convection. Instead of individual holes, you may like to cut out large square holes and cover them with fine mesh. Because lizards can escape through very small openings, it probably is safest to securely cover any ventilation holes, regardless of size, with fine wire mesh. Narrow wooden beading may be framed around the edges of the mesh to give a neat effect. A sliding metal, plastic, or wooden tray can be fitted in the base of the box to hold the substrate and facilitate cleaning.

GLASS TERRARIA

Ordinary aquarium tanks often are used to keep lizards. These are perfectly all right to use providing you ensure adequate ventilation. With silicone rubber sealer, it is possible to build glass terraria in many shapes and sizes. By using a combination of glass and acrylic (Plexiglas) materials, you can still have ventilation holes drilled in the sides or back. Glass is extremely good for making humid terraria or aqua-terraria in which part or all of the floor is to be water. The lid for a glass terrarium should preferably be made of plywood or plastic and should be elevated to form a cavity in which the heating and lighting apparatus

can be concealed from view from the outside. It is best to cover the apparatus with wire mesh so the inmates cannot gain access to it and burn themselves.

TERRARIUM DECORATIONS AND FURNISHINGS

Indoor terraria require various furnishings that are both functional and decorative. Although it is possible to keep and breed lizards in almost "clinical" conditions (a sheet of absorbent paper, a water dish, and a hide box), most

herpetologists require their terraria to be decorative and "simulate" to some extent natural conditions. The clinical or "sterile" method can still be convenient if you want to keep several breeding pairs or colonies and are not especially interested in observing semi-natural behavior.

Substrate Materials:

Floor coverings are many and varied. Coarse sand can be used for a desert terrarium, while a mixture of peat, sand, and loam can be used in woodland terraria. For larger, robust species it is best to use washed gravel, which can be obtained in various grades. Do not use very fine sand, as it tends to cake between the lizard's scales. For burrowing species, a mixture of coarse sand and leaf litter can be used. Whatever substrate material you use, it must be removed for washing, sterilization, and drying or it must be replaced at regular intervals. Cleaning is of course more frequent for larger species with copious droppings.

Rocks:

Rocks of interesting shapes and colors are not only decorative in the terrarium, but they are used as basking sites, as hiding places, and as an aid to shedding. You may buy suitable rocks in your local pet store or go out and find your own. Always make sure the rocks are placed firmly and cannot fall down and injure the reptiles. When large piles of rocks are used it is best to cement them together, leaving a few controllable hiding places.

Tree Branches and Logs:

For arboreal species, a few tree branches are indispensable. It is more practical to use a dead tree branch and grow a creeping house plant on it than to try and grow a tree or shrub in the terrarium. Try to select branches with interesting shapes. Driftwood collected from the sea shore or from river banks is often attractive as it will have been weathered by the action of sand, sun, and water. All wood used should be thoroughly scrubbed, rinsed, and dried before being used. You may want to immerse the log in a solution of bleach for a day or two to give it a more weathered appearance.

Plants:

There is no doubt that healthy, living plants in the terrarium provide an important esthetic touch. Unless the terrarium is very large, it is futile to try and grow plants where large, robust lizards are being kept, as they will be continually uprooted or flattened. Likewise, herbivorous lizards will eat most plants before they get a chance to become established. In such cases, however unesthetic it may seem, we have to compromise by using sturdy plastic plants or we must do without plants. For small lizards, the terrarium may be attractively planted. Select plant species compatible to the type of environment in the terrarium. Many common house plants are suitable, so it might be useful to study a good book on house-plant culture to aid in your selection.

Plants are best left in pots, which can be concealed behind rocks or in special cavities in logs or rockwork. It is then easy to remove and replace them should they begin to fail. It is advisable to have spare potted plants in similar sized pots so they can be changed at, say, monthly intervals or at cleaning time. The plant that has suffered the rigors of terrarium life can then be given a period of rest and recuperation in the greenhouse or on the window sill until its partner requires similar first aid.

LIFE SUPPORT SYSTEMS

Indoor terraria have to be provided with artificial life supports to compensate for the lack of natural ones. Such systems include heating, lighting, humidity, and ventilation. The first three factors will vary from species to species, but ventilation is important for all lizards at all times.

Heating

Being poikilothermic or "cold-blooded," lizards maintain their body heat at a preferred temperature by moving in and out of warm places, by basking directly in the sun, and/or by absorbing heat from require a reduction in temperature at night. In the home, this can be accomplished by simply switching off the heat source and allowing the terrarium to cool to room temperature.

TUNGSTEN LAMPS:

Ordinary household tungsten

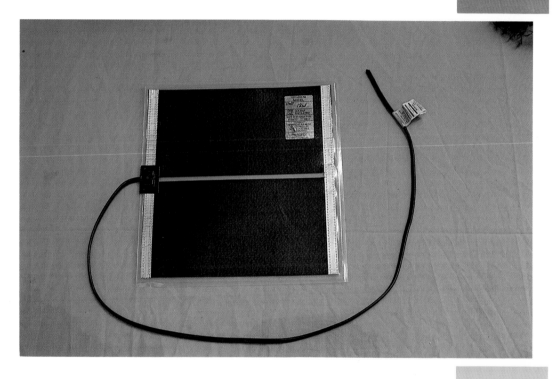

sun-warmed soil, rocks, or other items. Using natural sunlight through terrarium glass poses problems of overheating, so artificial means of heating usually are employed. Temperatures required by individual species vary considerably. Remember that apart from those inhabiting lowland equatorial areas, most species lamps had long been used as a sole source of heating and lighting in the home terrarium until it was discovered that the quality of light emitted was insufficient for diurnal basking lizards. However, tungsten bulbs should not be totally ignored. They are inexpensive, emit a fair amount of heat, and will supply supplementary light. The volume of

7

the terrarium will dictate what wattage of lamp(s) to use. By experimenting with various wattages and a thermometer, suitable temperatures will be arrived at. A tungsten lamp may be concealed inside a flowerpot or metal canister and controlled by a thermostat so a constant minimum background temperature is maintained.

SPOT LAMPS:

Various kinds of spot lamps are available that produce either infrared or white radiant heat. These are useful for directing at basking areas. They should preferably be set at one end of the terrarium only so there is a temperature gradient from one end of the cage to the other. The lizards will then be able to seek out their own preferred temperatures. Special ceramic heaters also are available. These emit heat but no light and are useful for maintaining background heat at night.

AQUARIUM HEATERS:

For humid terraria, an aquarium heater placed in the water will keep both water and air warm and provide needed humidity. The addition of an aquarium aerator will increase humidity even more and will help raise the air temperature, provide additional ventilation, and help keep the water fresh.

OTHER HEATERS:

Used for heating parts of the substrate, cable heaters or pads can be employed to provide further basking areas. There is always a chance of electrical shock with these devices, however, so caution is urged, especially in humid terraria. Most pads are put under the terrarium, while heating cables must be buried where the lizards will not dig them up and chew on them. A "hot rock" heater is often recommended as both a basking spot and supplemental heater. It consists of a heating element of some type embedded in a plaster block. Be sure to follow manufacturer's instructions closely when using this type of heater, as the potential for shocks exists.

Lighting

Natural sunlight or a good substitute is essential to the well-being of all diurnal lizards. The ultraviolet rays are important as they help stimulate the manufacture of vitamin D3 in the skin. This vitamin is essential for controlling the action of the important minerals calcium and phosphorus in the body, and without it various health problems will ensue. By all means allow your lizards to have unfiltered natural sunlight if possible by allowing it to pass through mesh. Natural sunlight filtered through glass is not beneficial, as the ultraviolet rays are cut out. In cooler temperate areas it is impossible to place terraria outside for most of the year, so compromise lighting of good quality must be provided. Broad-spectrum fluorescent tubes that emit "blue" light will provide sufficient ultraviolet light for your lizards. Be aware that too much ultraviolet light can be as damaging than too little. Research into suitable light sources for aquaria and terraria is continuing, and information on suitable systems may be obtained from a pet shop that specializes in reptiles.

Humidity

Lizards from damp areas require the atmosphere to be humid, while others may require seasonal increases in humidity. The maintenance of high humidity in the terrarium is quite easy if aquarium heaters are used in the water dish. Alternatively, the heater can be placed in a concealed jar of water that is topped up as necessary. An aerator used in the water will further increase the humidity and air temperature and is ideal for use in tropical rainforest terraria. An attractive little waterfall or seepage area can be created by using an airlift filter in conjunction with the aerator. One simple method of maintaining humidity in a plánted terrarium is to use a fine mist-sprayer containing lukewarm water

two or three times a day.

Many lizards require a very dry atmosphere with very low humidity. In cooler temperate climes that condition may be very hard to duplicate, making it difficult to keep certain desert species. Mesh lids on terraria reduce condensation and humidity within the tank, as does the absence of broad-leaved plants.

Water bowls should be no larger than necessary, the substrate must be kept fresh and dry, and warm, dry basking areas must be maintained.

Ventilation

Inadequate ventilation in the terrarium will lead to a buildup of stagnant air and an excess of carbon dioxide, providing favorable conditions for disease organisms. Additionally, a badly ventilated humid terrarium will develop

Many styles of "hot rocks" are available, some more dependable than others. Photo: S. & H. Miller.

unpleasant growths of molds and other fungi. It therefore is important to ensure that there is a constant air exchange in the terrarium, but without creating cold drafts. In most cases, the provision of adequate ventilation holes in the sides and top of a terrarium is all that is required. The warmth generated by the heating apparatus will cause air convection currents, the warm air leaving through the top and fresh air replacing it through the side vents. In terraria of lizards requiring humid surroundings, an aquarium aerator operated from a small air pump can be used to supply extra ventilation.

Where a terrarium is situated in a stuffy living room, particularly where the owners are smokers, it is recommended that the air inlet be placed outside the room. In cold weather, the air tube can be laid near a baseboard heater or radiator so the chill will be removed from it before it enters the terrarium.

Safety Precautions

As the heating and lighting equipment is operated by electricity, you should take adequate safety precautions to avoid electrical accidents. Unless you are an adept electrician, use only equipment that has passed relevant safety standards and use it according to the manufacturer's instructions. If in doubt, employ a qualified electrician to do your wiring and installing. Remember that electricity and water form a dangerous combination!

Curlytails, *Leiocephalus schreibersi*, require a warm but dry cage without crowding. Photo: G. Dingerkus.

Foods and Feeding

Until comparatively recently, the nutritional requirements of captive reptiles have been poorly understood research into the nutrition of reptiles can be described as "incidentally scientific." There is a certain

and mainly speculative, based on our knowledge of what the particular species is known to eat in the wild coupled with what we know about the nutritional husbandry of domestic animals. Research into the latter is, of course, a matter of "economic necessity," while similarity between the nutritional requirements of domestic fowl and reptiles, but a major variant is that reptiles do not have the high energy requirement of fowl to maintain a constantly high body temperature (i.e., chickens do not have to bask in sunlight).

The delicate banded gecko, *Coleonyx variegatus.* **Photo: K. T. Nemuras.**

However, the increase in popularity of lizards and other reptiles as pets over the past few decades has led to research into the nutrition of these animals, at least by some scientists. Coupled with the vast amount of nutritional knowledge assembled over the years by amateur and professional herpetologists, this has led to a situation where no captive lizard needs to be deficient in any dietary item.

We have known for a relatively long time that, to remain in the best of health and in prime condition, all animals must receive a balanced diet. A balanced diet consists of a number of primary nutritional constituents taken in appropriate amounts. These primary constituents are **proteins** (for the growth, repair, and replacement of body tissues as well as many other biological and metabolic functions); **carbohydrates** (for immediate energy requirements); **fats** (for stored energy requirements and insulation); **minerals**, particularly calcium and phosphorus (for bone growth and repair, proper function of the cell membranes, and the buffering of body fluids); **vitamins** (various essential functions); and, finally, **water** (the elixir of life).

Unfortunately, different species not only acquire these dietary constituents in different ways, but they may require them in various percentages. It can be safely assumed that each lizard species in the wild obtains its balanced diet requirements by feeding upon the type and variety of food items available in its natural habitat. Remember that a species will have lived in that habitat for thousands (maybe millions) of years, and there will be a very close relationship between it and the food available. We still have insufficient data on what most individual species eat in the wild. We may see a wild lizard catch a grasshopper, but this does not mean that grasshoppers are its sole food or even its main food.

In some cases analysis of fecal samples from free-living reptiles has given an insight into what the animals eat. Unfortunately, the only sure way of analyzing the diet of a wild population of a particular species is to catch a large number of them and systematically examine their stomach contents over a number of seasons. Once this required that the lizards be killed and the stomachs removed, but now this often is done by flushing the stomach with water, stressful perhaps but not fatal. Even then, the knowledge we may gain of wild diets may not necessarily help us. It will certainly be impossible to provide our captives with the exact type and variety of foods they take in the wild. Thus we are obliged to provide substitutes.

Lizards can be split into three main groups depending on the type of food they eat.

CARNIVOROUS: Feeding on animal material (in its widest sense),

ranging from small invertebrates to larger vertebrates depending on the size of the lizard. This is by far the largest group.

HERBIVOROUS: Feeding almost exclusively on plant material.

OMNIVOROUS: Feeding on a fairly equal mixture of plant and animal tissues.

These groups are far from clear-cut. A carnivore swallowing a whole prey animal will also be swallowing the contents of that animal's stomach, which may include a high proportion of plant material. Conversely, a herbivore will consume a fair proportion of the animal life that is associated with the plant material it eats. One of the most important considerations to be taken into account when feeding captive reptiles is that "variety is the spice of life," although some species require more variety in their diet than others. Before selecting a particular species of lizard to keep, you should first ascertain whether a continuous supply of appropriate food items will be available. The feeding requirements of various species are given with the species descriptions later, but the following gives some general ideas on the types of foods available.

COLLECTING LIVE FOODS

Although there are several kinds

of live foods that can be purchased at regular intervals or propagated in the home, the collection of a varied supply from the wild is highly recommended. This may be difficult if you live in the city and not very productive during the winter in colder climates, but it is worth making the effort. An hour or so spent collecting insects and other items during a summer weekend trip into the countryside can be very productive. A mixture of wild-caught invertebrates will not only provide your captives with a greater variety of diet, it will also help relieve boredom to a certain extent; lizards are likely to fast if continually given the same old items on the menu.

Perhaps the most productive method of obtaining a selection of terrestrial insects and spiders is "sweeping." This is accomplished by passing a large, fine-meshed net through the foliage of trees, shrubs, and tall grass. Special sweep nets are available through biological supply houses, but ordinary butterfly nets can be used, especially if reinforced with canvas around the rim to help prevent ripping. Such sweeping in the summer months will provide quantities of beetles, moths, caterpillars, grasshoppers, and spiders, all items that most insectivorous lizards will eagerly accept. The insects can be placed in a number of jars or small plastic containers for transport home. Do not put too many insects into the terrarium at any one time—allow the lizards to consume what is available before adding more, otherwise you will get escapes into the house.

Another good method of collecting live foods is to search under rotten logs, rocks, and other debris. Damp areas will produce large numbers of beetles, woodlice, and earthworms. By breaking open rotten timber, you will find the grubs of many insects. In some countries termites are easily found; the soft, white bodies of these "white ants" make them an excellent food for many lizards.

During the summer months you will find the flower garden an excellent hunting ground for small insects. Tiny beetles and flies (especially useful for very small or juvenile lizards) congregate among the petals of flowers and can be collected using a "pooter." This consists of a glass or plastic bottle containing a cork through which two glass tubes are passed. One of the tubes has a piece of rubber tubing about 6 inches (15 cm) long attached to it. The insects are caught by placing the end of the rubber tube into the corolla of the flower and sucking sharply on the other tube with the mouth. The insects will be pulled through the long tube and fall into the bottle. A piece of fine mesh placed over the bottom end of the mouthpiece tube will prevent unfortunate accidents.

Aphids, the bane of the gardener in the summer, are another useful food item for very small lizards. These little insects are often found in great numbers on the new green shoots of plants. By simply breaking off a whole infested shoot and placing it in the terrarium, you will have a ready supply of food for your tiny lizards. (Putting the shoot into a small jar of water will keep it green longer and perhaps make more aphids available longer as well.)

Moths and other nocturnal insects can be caught in great quantities by using a light-trap. A white sheet is hung up in a suitable place and a strong light shone upon it. The insects will be attracted to the sheet and easily caught and placed in a container. A few specialized lizard species feed largely on ants, a food item that is rarely difficult to obtain, at least in the summer.

a powdered vitamin and mineral supplement added to the insects will considerably improve their nutritive value. The fine grains of the powder will adhere to the bodies of slightly dampened mealworms and will be taken in by the lizards as they feed. In many countries, mealworms are readily available from specialist

This gorgeous tropical grasshopper would be likely prey for lizards in the wild. Photo: P. Freed.

CULTURING LIVE FOODS
Mealworms:

For many years, mealworms were the staple diet of captive insectivorous pets. Mealworms are the larvae of the flour beetle *Tenebrio molitor*. Although mealworms are known to be fairly nutritious, they should be used only as a part of a varied diet. In particular, they tend to be deficient in calcium and certain vitamins, but

suppliers and can be purchased in small quantities at regular intervals. Alternatively, having purchased your first batch, you can breed your own stock. A dozen or so mealworms are placed in a shallow plastic or metal tray or box containing a 2-inch (5-cm) layer of bran or oatmeal covered with a piece of burlap or coarse cloth. One or two chunks of carrot or apple (changed

15

every couple of days) placed on the sacking will provide moisture for the insects. Keep the box covered but do not allow the humidity to condense inside the culture. Best results will be obtained if you maintain your cultures at 25-30°C (77-86°F). Each month, a further culture is started with a few beetles from the first culture, until you have four cultures at various stages of development. The worms in the first culture will pupate and emerge as adult beetles ready to mate, lay eggs, and repeat the cycle. After about eight weeks, you will have a new generation of mealworms. By constantly maintaining four cultures at various stages of development and replacing old cultures after two months or so, you will have mealworms of varying sizes, pupae, and adult beetles, all of which can be used as food for insectivorous lizards.

Crickets:

Cultures of these insects have become readily available through the pet trade in recent years. They are a highly nutritious source of food for captive lizards. Though there are many species of cricket, the one most commonly cultured is *Gryllus bimaculatus*. The crickets may be kept in small containers (an old leaky aquarium is ideal) with rolls of corrugated cardboard, pieces of crumpled newspaper, or old egg boxes in which they can hide. A small saucer containing a piece of wet cotton wool will provide drinking water for the insects. They may be fed on bran and the occasional piece of greenfood. The adult crickets are most likely to lay their eggs in damp sand or vermiculite, so a dish or two of this should be provided.

Any grasshopper or cricket that can be bred in captivity or collected in the wild probably will be eaten by lizards of the appropriate size. Photo: P. Freed.

The dish should be removed to a separate container at regular intervals and replaced with a new one. If kept at a temperature of about 25°C (77°F), the eggs will hatch in about three weeks. The newly hatched nymphs are about an eighth of an inch (3 mm) long and are very suitable food for tiny hatchling lizards. There are four instars (nymphal stages), each one a little larger in body than the former, providing various sizes for your lizards. The final adult size is about a bit over half an inch (15 mm). A carefully planned and harvested breeding colony of crickets will provide a constant supply of excellent live food throughout the year.

To remove crickets from their container, pick up a piece of the cardboard in which they are hiding and shake the insects out into a jar. If placed in the refrigerator for ten minutes or so, the insects will be subdued enough to prevent escapes when feeding them to your lizards.

Flies:

Various species of fly are suitable food for lizards both in the larval and adult form. Fruitflies (*Drosophila*), tiny black insects that congregate and breed in rotten fruit, are an excellent food for the hatchlings of very small lizard

species. A colony can soon be started (in the summer) by placing a box of banana skins or rotten fruit in a remote corner of the garden, where it soon will be teeming with flies. The little flies can be captured using a fine meshed net and transferred directly to the terrarium. Due to their fast breeding cycle, fruitflies are used extensively in genetics research. University genetics classes often culture them in jars of agar jelly and can often be persuaded to part with a few cultures and instructions on their further proliferation. Cultures are also sold by biological supply houses and some pet shops. The housefly (*Musca*) is another excellent food for smaller lizards, while the bigger greenbottle and bluebottle (*Lucilia* and *Calliphora*) species may be suitable for larger lizards. Flies collected in jars can be subdued by placing them in the refrigerator for ten minutes or so, thus reducing the incidence of escapes when you add them to the terrarium.

Vestigial-winged fruitflies are commonly cultured as food for small lizards. Photo: M. Gilroy.

Earthworms:

Although many lizards will not eat earthworms, they are an excellent and nutritious food for those that will. Cultures of various earthworm species are available from bait shops and some pet shops, though if you have a garden it is quite easy to find your own supply. A good method of obtaining a fairly continuous supply of earthworms during the warmer months is to clear a patch of soil in some corner of the garden, preferably where it is shaded from the sun. Place a 2-inch (5-cm) layer of dead leaves or grass clippings over the patch and cover this with a piece of burlap (pegged down to prevent it from blowing away). This should be kept moist by regular watering. Earthworms will soon congregate in the rotting vegetation below the sacking and can easily be collected.

Mice and Rats:

Larger lizards (varanids, teiids, some iguanids and agamids, etc.) require more substantial food than invertebrates. The availability of laboratory mice and rats makes these animals an almost required diet for many captive reptiles. Providing they have themselves been reared on a balanced diet, rodents are a balanced diet in themselves for larger carnivorous lizards. It is up to the individual whether he wants to breed his supply of mice and rats or to purchase a supply as necessary. Mice and rats can be purchased from pet shops dealing heavily in reptiles. They may be available deep-frozen, perhaps the most simple way of storing and the safest way of feeding.

Chicks:

The young chicks of domestic fowl may be obtained inexpensively from hatcheries either alive or dead (sometimes deep-frozen). Chicks that have started to grow and are a few days old are more nutritious than hatchlings.

VEGETABLE FOODS

Many lizard species, especially iguanids, are almost wholly or at least partially herbivorous and will take varying amounts of vegetable matter. Even some species generally considered to be carnivorous will occasionally take soft fruits and grated vegetables. Most of the usual domestic fruits and vegetables are suitable, and by experimenting with a variety of foods a feeding strategy can be formulated. Lettuce, cabbage (shredded), carrot (grated), tomatoes, peppers, cucumbers, apples, pears, bananas, grapes, oranges, boiled potatoes, and various other items can be tried out. Some particularly fussy feeders may require a whole range of experimentation before you reach a satisfactory feeding regimen. Fickle feeders are often tempted with such items as fresh strawberries, canned peaches, or canned peas. Species such as the desert iguana, *Dipsosaurus dorsalis*, which feeds on pungent desert plants in the wild, may often be tempted with plants such as mint or rosemary from the herb garden.

OTHER FOODS

Some carnivorous lizards, especially those species that feed regularly on carrion in the wild, will eagerly accept pieces of lean meat, heart, or liver (minced for the smaller individuals). If mixed with raw egg (including the finely crushed shell), the meat may be even more eagerly accepted. Canned dog or cat food may also be accepted by many species. Some large monitor lizards will swallow chicken eggs shell and all, while smaller ones can be given pigeon or quail eggs.

SUPPLEMENTS

Lean meat should never be fed as a staple diet as it lacks the important roughage of bones, fur, or feathers. If it becomes necessary to give lean meat for extended periods (due to a shortage of mice, rats, or chicks, for example), then a suitable vitamin and mineral supplement must be added. Powdered supplements can be quite easily added to the meat and rubbed into it. Ask your veterinarian or enquire at your pet shop about which brands are most suitable. One should ensure that a range of vitamins is available, as well as minerals, especially calcium and phosphorous compounds. Supplements should be given to all insectivorous and herbivorous lizards on a regular basis (say twice

per week) by sprinkling the powder onto the food.

FEEDING STRATEGIES

Small lizard species and juveniles of larger ones generally require to feed more often than large lizards. Small insectivores and all herbivores should be fed daily, while most of the larger carnivorous lizards will get by on two or three sizable meals per week. It is difficult to lay down any hard and fast rules regarding quantities. You should aim at keeping the diet balanced without over-feeding (obesity is a common cause of premature death in captive reptiles), and a certain amount of experimentation will be required before you arrive at a suitable routine.

Mealworms are a standard lizard food but should not be fed exclusively or to small lizards. Photo: M. Gilroy.

General Care and Health

The standards of care and health of pet lizards are closely related subjects that go hand in hand. Bad management and poor hygiene will soon lead to sickness and even death of your lizards. Hygiene is the art or science of disease prevention or, conversely, the preservation of good health. This is not quite as difficult as it may sound.

STRESS

A good hygienic practice is to provide the animals with all they require to prevent stress. Most lizards are not very adaptable to surroundings that are alien to them, so sudden or prolonged changes in temperature, humidity, diet, or even terrain can cause stress that reduces resistance to disease. Many disease organisms may be present in the animals themselves, in the air, in the drinking water, and in the food. Normal, healthy lizards kept in a stress-free environment will have immune systems in operation that will prevent disease organisms from invading the body. In stressed animals the immune systems may fail, resulting in an outbreak of disease that could otherwise have been combated.

SELECTION OF SPECIMENS

Having decided on what species to keep, the next step is to select individual specimens. Perhaps surprisingly, this is an important aspect of hygiene, as one should ensure that the acquired stock is healthy in the first place. When purchasing from a pet shop, for example, first impressions of the premises can give you a good idea as to the likely state of the animals in stock. Stores and cages that are smelly, dirty, and untidy and are overstocked are more likely to nurture disease organisms than establishments whose proprietors obviously spend time to provide all necessary requirements and display the animals in a way designed to impress the customer. A pet shop keeper should have pride in his chosen trade and not be just out to make a quick buck. If you are not impressed with the standard of health in a dealer's store, pass him by and go where you are more likely to obtain healthy stock.

As with any financial transaction, you must ensure you are getting value for your money. It is, however, better to pay a little more for a healthy specimen than to "save" a few dollars on a suspect one. Examine each specimen very carefully before making your selection. Look for signs of ticks and mites on the skin, especially around the vent, near the base of the limbs, and in the folds around the neck. Choose lizards that have a clean, unbroken skin devoid of any old unshed patches. With a little practice you will be able to tell if a lizard is shedding healthily, in which case there is no reason to reject it. Ensure that the reptile is alert, clear-eyed, and plump; do not select specimens that are excessively thin (hollow-bellied, ribs visible through the skin, emaciated tail, etc.). Find out from the dealer if the animal is feeding regularly and what it is feeding on. Examine the mouth and vent for signs of inflammation or discharges that could indicate disease. Most dealers will allow prospective buyers to handle stock for the purpose of inspection.

Apart from purchasing lizards from pet shops or from specialist dealers in reptiles, there are a couple of other ways of obtaining specimens. One very good source is from the amateur hobbyist who has already succeeded in breeding his

Some lizards are too delicate to keep in captivity long, like *Chamaeleo montium*. Photo: P. Freed.

specimens and has surplus juvenile stock for disposal. A great advantage of such "captive-bred" (CB) specimens is that they are already accustomed to terrarium life, as they may have been handled from an early age and will be "used" to people. Captive-bred stock tends to be healthier than wild-caught specimens, often is easier to explain legally if the restrictions imposed in your area are strict, and are less damaging to natural populations than repeated collecting of wild specimens for the hobby. CB lizards often represent species that are rare or even threatened in nature or have very limited ranges. Such species are unavailable or very expensive as wild-caught specimens and may not be keepable because of endangered species laws. The great number of species being bred in captivity and made available through small-scale mail order dealers has brought about a resurgence of interest in the terrarium hobby in these environmentally active days. Your local herp society (contact the closest museum, zoo, or university zoology department for an address) often will have listings of suppliers or may carry classified ads with such material offered for sale.

The final method of acquisition, collection from the wild, is one that should be considered with great caution. In many countries, all lizard species are protected by law and must not be interfered with in any way. In some countries, only licensed collectors are allowed to capture specimens. In other cases only certain species may be protected, while others may be collected by unlicensed persons. Before embarking on a collecting trip, ensure that you find out the appropriate legislation pertaining to the country, state, or area in which you intend to work. Do not indiscriminately collect large numbers of lizards even if the laws should allow it—take only what you can comfortably house. In most cases a single pair or minimal breeding group should suffice.

QUARANTINE

Before adding new lizards to an existing collection, they should undergo a period of quarantine to prevent diseases being introduced to the existing stock. They should be placed in a simple cage (preferably in a room separate from the main collection), fed and watered, and kept under close observation for not less than 21 days. If no obvious symptoms of disease develop in this period, it should be safe to introduce the lizards to those already in collection.

HANDLING

The subject of handling is often a controversial one. Some herpetologists maintain that lizards should be handled as little as possible as it is an "unnatural" experience for the reptiles and could have an adverse effect on health and breeding ability. Others say that regular handling (usually for the

pleasure of the owner) is necessary to keep the reptiles "used" to people and to keep them tame and trusting. Whatever you may think, there will always be times when it becomes necessary to handle lizards for one reason or another. Methods of handling lizards will vary, depending on their size and aggressiveness. Many will quickly become tame and easy to handle, particularly if reared from birth, while others may retain an aggressive streak throughout their lives.

Small lizards up to about 8 inches (20 cm) in total length may be grasped firmly but gently just behind the head with the thumb and forefinger, while placing the remainder of the hand gently around the body. Never pick up a lizard by the tail, as many species will shed the tail at the slightest provocation. Although small lizards will often attempt to bite, they are not strong enough to cause any serious injury and the skin is unlikely to be broken.

Lizards in the medium range (say 8-20 inches, 20-50 cm, total length) should be grasped around the thoracic region of the body, restraining the head with the thumb and forefinger. Particularly lively specimens can be further restrained by holding the hindquarters with the other hand. Medium-sized lizards may be capable of giving painful bites, but these are only likely to cause minor breaks in the skin that can be treated with antiseptic.

Lizards in excess of 20 inches (50

The tail of this *Eumeces fasciatus* partially broke and then regenerated a large twin to the side. Photo: K. Lucas.

cm) total length—and in particular large iguanids, teiids, and varanids—can give deep, painful bites and can also scratch with their powerful claws. They should be grasped firmly around the neck with one hand and around the waist with the other. The tail and hindlimbs can be restrained by hugging them to the body with the elbow. When handling large lizards it is best to wear old clothes in case of damage by the claws or soiling by the feces of nervous specimens, which are likely to void the contents of the cloaca when restrained. One salient point to remember is that a good herpetologist *never* gets bitten by his reptiles.

CLEANING

In order to minimize the risk of disease outbreaks, terraria should be kept spotlessly clean. For simple terraria, absorbent paper (such as newspaper) can be used as a substrate and changed each time it becomes soiled. With other forms of substrate, fecal pellets can be removed using a spoon or small shovel. About once per month the whole terrarium should be cleaned and the substrate and decorations removed and either discarded or sterilized and then scrubbed clean. The interior of the terrarium and its contents should be scrubbed with warm soapy water and a mild disinfectant such as bleach or povidone-iodine, then thoroughly rinsed with clean water before being dried and refurnished.

During cleaning operations the reptiles can be placed in a spare cage or a plastic box. A plastic trash can is useful for large species. Water for drinking and/or bathing should be changed very regularly, preferably daily or more often if necessary. The glass viewing panels should also be kept crystal clear.

HIBERNATION

The importance of hibernation to many lizard species cannot be overstressed. Lizards from temperate and subtropical climates usually hibernate for varying periods of time, depending on the ambient temperatures. In the wild, lizards seek out hibernation spots far enough below ground to be unaffected by frost. Many species can withstand amazingly low temperatures provided they do not freeze. The period of hibernation is a part of the life cycle that helps bring some reptiles into breeding condition. In the past many captive lizards were kept active in high temperatures throughout the year. The general opinion now is that non-tropical lizards should be given varying periods of artificial hibernation to enhance their lives and increase the prospects of breeding. A hibernating "pet" lizard may seem boring as it will not be seen for quite a long period, but a short "rest-period" at lower temperatures seems to be an adequate substitute for full hibernation.

Only healthy, well-fed specimens

should be hibernated. Reduce and then stop feeding it while gradually reducing the temperature over a period of several days. The minimum temperature will vary from 39°F (4°C) for cold-temperate species to 50°F (10°C) for subtropical species. The photoperiod can also be reduced at the same time. The animals should be kept at these temperatures in an unheated but frost-free room for periods ranging from 4-12 weeks depending on their natural climatic zones. After the "rest-period," the reverse procedure should be used to bring the temperature and photoperiod back to "summertime."

DISEASES AND TREATMENT

Lizards kept hygienically in a stress-free environment and receiving an adequate diet will remain remarkably resistant to disease. Many outbreaks of disease can be related to some inadequacy in the captive management, so careful thought must be applied at all times in providing their needs. If it is suspected that all is not well with your lizards, a veterinarian should be consulted. Though many veterinarians are inexperienced in reptile medicine, most will be able to put you in touch with one who is. Some of the more usual problems are described below.

Egernia depressa **is a skink now widely bred in captivity and virtually without diseases. Photo: R. D. Bartlett.**

Nutritional Problems:

A common cause of sickness in many captive lizards can be put down to a deficiency in certain dietary constituents. With a variety of the right types of food, vitamin and mineral supplements, and an opportunity to bask in sunlight or artificial sunlight, the incidence of such conditions will be minimized.

Wounds and Injuries:

Though not strictly diseases, wounds caused by fighting, attempting to escape, etc., are susceptible to infection and must be treated. Shallow wounds will usually heal automatically if swabbed daily with a mild antiseptic such as povidone-iodine. Deeper or badly infected wounds should be treated by a veterinarian as in some cases surgery and suturing may be required.

Ectoparasites:

These are parasites that attack external areas of the body in order to suck blood. Ticks and mites are the most usual external parasites associated with lizards. Ticks are often found attached to newly captured specimens and may range up to almost a quarter-inch (6 mm) in length. They fasten themselves with their piercing mouthparts to the lizard's skin, usually in a secluded spot between scales, often around the vent, below the neck, or where the limbs join the body. Do not attempt to pull a tick out directly, as its head may be left embedded in the skin, causing an infection later. The tick's body should first be dabbed with a little alcohol to relax the mouthparts. The tick can then be gently pulled out with thumb and forefinger or with forceps. Once all ticks are removed from a wild caught specimen, a further infestation in the terrarium is unlikely. Mites are more serious as they can multiply to large numbers in the terrarium before they are even noticed. They do not necessarily stay on the reptile's body all of the time but may hide in crevices in the terrarium. In great numbers, mites can cause stress, anemia, shedding problems, loss of appetite, and eventual death. They are also capable of transmitting pathogenic organisms in the blood from one reptile to another. The individual reptile mite is smaller than a pin-head, roughly globular in shape, and grayish in color, becoming red after it has partaken of a blood meal. In a heavily infested terrarium, the mites may be seen running over the surfaces, particularly at "lights-on" in the mornings, and their powdery silver droppings may be seen on the lizard's skin. Mites are most often introduced to the terrarium with new stock (another good reason for quarantine and careful inspection).

Fortunately, mites can be quickly eradicated by using a dichlorvos-impregnated plastic strip of the type used to control houseflies. A small piece of such a strip placed in a perforated container and suspended in the terrarium will kill off free-moving mites. Remove the strip after three days then repeat the operation ten days later to kill off any newly hatched mites. Two or three treatments will usually destroy all mites in the terrarium. Unfortunately, these strips have been removed from the market in some areas and are considered dangerous to humans by some scientists. A dehydrating powder for the control of mites should be available through your dealer if other chemicals are unavailable. As a last resort, the lizard can be submerged in warm water with only the nostrils exposed, hopefully submerging any mites on its body; the cage of course must be sterilized at the same time. Submerging is very stressful for many lizards, large lizards may be difficult to hold for ten or 15 minutes in a waterbath, and mites are hard to kill this way.

Mites are possible on any lizard. *Phelsuma cepediana.* Photo: J. Visser.

Endoparasites:

These are organisms that live inside the body, usually in the alimentary tract. The ones with which the lizard keeper is most likely to be concerned are roundworms and tapeworms. Wild lizards are nearly all infected with worms of one form or another, and in most cases there is no real danger to the reptiles. However, during times of stress (capture, for example), normal resistance to the worms will be reduced, triggering a massive increase in size or numbers of worms and often leading to anemia, general lethargy, loss of appetite, and even death. Routine microscopic examination of fecal samples in a veterinary laboratory will reveal infestations. There are several proprietary brands of vermicides available through your veterinarian that may be offered with the food or, in severe cases, via stomach tube.

Bacterial Infections:

There are many forms of bacterial infections that can affect lizards, especially in unhygienic conditions. Infective salmonellosis is an intestinal disease that has been known to have been transmitted from reptiles to man (especially so from freshwater turtles), so it is important to thoroughly wash the hands after each cleaning or handling session. In lizards, salmonellosis manifests itself in watery, green-colored, foul-odored feces. Consult a veterinarian if you suspect the condition. He will probably treat the infection with antibiotics.

Protozoan Infections:

Various enteric infections can be caused by protozoans, including *Entamoeba invadens*. If untreated, the disease can rapidly reach epidemic proportions in captive reptiles. Symptoms include watery, slimy feces and general debilitation. Treatment with metronidazole (by a veterinarian) via stomach tube has proved effective for this and other protozoan infections.

Skin Problems:

A common cause of skin infections in lizards is inability to shed properly, often as a result of a mite infestation or stress brought about by various other factors. Mite infestations should be cleared immediately and aid should be given to lizards experiencing difficulty in shedding. Most healthy lizards will shed (molt) their skins without problems several times per year, a natural phenomenon related to growth. The skin is normally shed in patches and the whole process should take no more than a few days. Disease organisms can grow behind persistent patches of old skin that do not come off readily. The skin can often be loosened and peeled off by placing the reptile in a bath of very shallow, warm water for an hour or so.

Abscesses:

These appear as lumps below the skin and are usually caused by an infection building up in the flesh after the skin has been accidentally damaged for one reason or another. Abscesses should be referred to a veterinarian, who will give antibiotic treatment. In severe cases the abscess may be surgically opened, cleaned, and then sutured.

Respiratory Infections:

Though relatively uncommon in lizards, respiratory infections may occur occasionally in stressed specimens. The patient will have difficulty in breathing, the nostrils will be blocked, and there will be a nasal discharge. Often the symptoms can be alleviated by moving the patient to a warmer, drier, well-ventilated terrarium. More serious cases will require antibiotic treatment from the veterinarian.

Breeding

REPRODUCTIVE CYCLES

Lizards are unable to adapt to climates significantly different from those of their native habitat, and no captive breeding will occur unless one attempts to reproduce these climates as closely as possible. The reproductive cycles of all species are to a greater or lesser extent affected by environment and seasonal changes. Before any attempt at captive breeding is contemplated, it is essential to be aware of the environmental conditions prevailing in the natural habitat of the species in question; the provision of the correct "seasonal changes" in the terrarium will greatly enhance the chances of successful breeding. On reaching maturity, most lizards from temperate climates breed once per year, while some of the smaller species from subtropical and tropical climates may breed twice or more. Temperate species have a relatively short time to complete their breeding cycle, so courtship activity must start as early as possible in the season. The period of hibernation plays an important part in preparing such species for breeding. In tropical species the breeding cycle may be affected by the onset of "wet" or "dry" periods; some may benefit from a period of estivation or changes in humidity. By using a combination of heaters, lamps, timers, and humidifiers, it is possible to reproduce a miniclimate suitable for the reproductive cycles of most species.

Most lizards live fairly solitary

A pair of mating *Phelsuma madagascariensis*, Madagascar day geckos. Photo: R. Heselhaus.

lives outside the breeding season, though there may be fairly active territorial interaction. Some species live in "gregarious colonies" (*Agama agama*, for example), often in a relatively small area such as a single tree or rocky outcrop. The strongest, or at least the most aggressive, male will take the highest point available and advertise his superiority by taking on bright colors and making bizarre body movements including head-bobbing, dewlap displays, and other activities, depending on specific behavior. The dominant male usually will have the choice of females, but he will have a hard job keeping competitors at bay, often temporarily losing his superior position to an interloper while defending it from yet another male.

A sexually aroused male lizard will often contort his body into bizarre shapes, ostensibly to make himself look more attractive. With arched or twisted body, outstretched limbs, and quivering tail, he will approach the female, which, more often than not, will be unimpressed by his efforts and may even take flight. The male will grab the female in the region of the neck, and if receptive she will submit; if not, she will fight him off. Having secured a receptive female, the male will maneuver his vent into apposition to hers before inserting one of his pair of hemipenes into her cloaca. Copulation can take minutes or hours, depending on the species and the circumstances. Lizard mating can appear to be excessively violent, but individuals are rarely injured and they should not be disturbed during the process.

SEX DETERMINATION

If you want to breed lizards, one of the most obvious requirements should be that you have at least one male and one female (there are a very few species that have been proven to be parthenogenetic, females being capable of producing offspring without being fertilized by a male). It is relatively easy to distinguish the sexes of most species due to differences in color, size, behavior, tail length and shape, and so on. However, there are some species that show no obvious sexual dimorphism. When dormant, the paired hemipenes of the male are inverted into cavities in the tail base. In many species this gives males an obvious swollen region in the base of the tail that contrasts strongly with the thinner tail base of the female.

A fairly recent method of sexing lizards and snakes, probing, has proven quite efficient. This is accomplished using a sexing probe manufactured from stainless steel or a hard synthetic and basically resemble knitting needles but with a small ball attached to the pointed end. Obtainable in various sizes from specialist suppliers, the probes are used by inserting the lubricated (use vaseline or mineral oil) ball-tip into either side of the vent and gently guiding the probe in the direction of the tail. In a male lizard the probe should enter the cavity formed by one of the inverted hemipenes and can be guided a relatively large distance. In the female, the probe will hardly travel any distance at all. Needless to say, the probe must not be forced and it may take a little practice before you become proficient. It may be advisable to get a more experienced herpetologist to give a demonstration before you attempt it yourself, as you are probing a very delicate area and can cause permanent damage from minor slips and miscalculations.

EGGLAYING AND BIRTH

Though most lizards lay eggs and are said to be oviparous, some species produce fully formed young at birth. In most cases this is a result of what is termed ovoviviparity, the eggs developing to full term in the mother's body and hatching just prior to or during deposition. Gravid females actively seek out suitable spots in

which to lay their eggs and seem to have an insight into the exact conditions required for hatching. Warmth and humidity seem to be the most important factors in incubation, so eggs are usually laid in excavations in a sunny spot over a moist substrate. An exception to this is most geckos, which lay their hard-shelled adhesive eggs in cracks in tree bark and similar situations. Concealment of the eggs from predators seems to be a prime consideration, as anyone who has tried to find wild lizard "nests" will tell you.

In an advanced state of pregnancy, gravid females take on a very plump appearance and the eggs may be seen, and palpated, as a series of bulges on either side of the abdomen. The period from mating to

Two hard eggs of a day gecko, *Phelsuma*. Most gecko eggs are glued to the surface. Photo: K. T. Nemuras.

egg-laying varies from species to species and also depends on various environmental factors. It may range from 30 days (or even less) to 100 days or more.

Gravid females should be given facilities for laying eggs in the terrarium. This can consist of trays filled with damp sand in which the reptiles will burrow. In the terrarium, lizards may not be satisfied with what you have to offer and may end up dropping the eggs indiscriminately over the substrate. Wherever eggs are laid in the terrarium, they are more likely to hatch if removed and artificially incubated. Once eggs are laid, the majority of species show no further interest in their offspring.

INCUBATION

The eggs of most lizard species (the geckos being an exception) have a white, leathery shell designed to absorb moisture from the substrate or incubation medium. Newly laid eggs often have dimples or collapsed areas, but these will soon fill out as moisture is absorbed. The eggs should be carefully removed (traditional practice requires that they should be kept the same way up as they were found and never be turned, but many keepers now believe that a little turning is harmless) and partially buried in an incubation medium contained in a shallow container. For convenience, the eggs can be laid in neat rows and buried to about two-thirds of their thickness. The exposed third allows

you to inspect the eggs without disturbing them.

Various experiments with all sorts of incubation media have been successful, but in the author's experience the most satisfactory method has been the use of granular vermiculite. This inert, sterile, absorbent insulating material is available in various grades. For general incubation purposes a fine grade is used. Mixed with about its own weight of water, the vermiculite will provide an ideal medium for incubation. The lid of the incubation box should have a few ventilation holes to allow for air circulation but not so many as to allow loss of moisture. The box is placed in a heated incubator and maintained at a suitable temperature. For most species temperatures in the range of 77-86°F (25-30°C) will be adequate.

The type of incubator appears to be unimportant as long as the correct temperature range can be provided. A simple wooden box containing an incandescent light bulb and a thermostat to regulate the temperature are all that are required, though more sophisticated appliances are available from specialist suppliers. With a thermometer in the box you will be able to monitor the temperature. It is best to use a blue bulb or to mount the bulb in some sort of cover to minimize light intensity. Alternatively, a heating pad, cable, or porcelain heater may be used.

During development, the eggs will absorb moisture from the

surrounding medium and increase in weight. Infertile eggs will not absorb water, but such eggs should not be discarded until you are absolutely certain they are not viable. Many keepers

hold eggs until they literally explode just to make sure there has not been just a temporary lapse in development. Incubation times will vary from species to species and may be anything from 30 to 100 days or more. This incubation time can be frustrating, and you may have a frequent desire to inspect the eggs or even to open one up to see if an embryo is developing. Patience is certainly a virtue here, however, and eventually one will hopefully be rewarded with a host of lively little offspring.

Most hatching lizards possess a sharp projection on the snout known as an egg-tooth or caruncle. This is used to slit open the tough, parchment-like shell at the time of hatching, but it is shed shortly afterward. Sometimes hatching lizards take a long time, often 24 hours or more, to actually leave the shell, but the temptation to "help" them is usually best suppressed unless the lizard is having obvious difficulties. Occasionally the egg fluids will harden, causing the little hatchling to adhere to the shell. This can be overcome by gently dabbing the affected parts with a bit of cotton soaked in lukewarm water.

REARING

Rearing some of the smaller species constitutes a challenge, the main problem being the maintenance of a constant supply of small insects for food. As soon as hatchlings are moving and detached from the egg shell, they should be

A female glass lizard, *Ophisaurus ventralis*, brooding her eggs, an occurrence rare among lizards. Photo: R. D. Bartlett.

removed from the incubation chamber and placed in a "nursery." This should be simply furnished but should have all the necessary life-support systems. Small species can be housed in small plastic tubs or boxes with ventilation holes drilled in the lid; a number of tubs can then be placed in a larger, heated terrarium. Do not attempt to remove the yolk sac, which will soon shrivel up, leaving a tiny scar on the belly.

Providing the conditions are correct and the food items acceptable, most lizards will start to feed shortly after hatching. If one kind of food is ignored, keep trying others until you are successful. Once a youngster starts taking one kind of food it will not be long before it is prepared to try others. It is a good idea to weigh your specimens regularly and monitor their growth. In any case, it is wise to keep records of the complete progress of your reptiles, both for your own use and for that of others in the future.

Popular Lizards

Lizards belong to the suborder Lacertilia of the order Squamata, which they share with the amphisbaenians and the snakes. Most herpetologists agree that the lizards fall into some 18 to 20 families with a total number of about 320 to 370 genera, over 3000 species, and many hundred valid subspecies. It is quite obvious that an introductory volume of this size could not possibly hope to cover more than a token number of genera, let alone species. In the following section a selection of species from better known or interesting genera is briefly discussed. Obviously these little discussions cannot be used for identification purposes, since so few species are included. Those requiring more detailed information on the recognition of individual species should refer to field guides for the appropriate areas.

The book *Breeding Terrarium Animals* by Zimmermann (T.F.H.) provides detailed coverage of captive care of most common and many uncommon lizards. *The Atlas of Reptiles and Amphibians for the*

Gonatodes humeralis, a tropical American gecko. Photo: P. Freed.

Terrarium by Obst, Richter, and Jacob (T.F.H.) is perhaps the ultimate reference source for information on most of the living amphibians and reptiles and their care in the terrarium; it is expensive but well worth the investment if you decide to go more deeply into the terrarium hobby.

I should provide the caveat that the following selection of basic lizards is only one possible grouping, representing what is currently available on the American

and European markets. Obviously local lizards will appear in pet shops from time to time and may make excellent pets, although not listed. Other lizards often considered as being fine for beginners, such as the green iguana, are ignored here because they are expensive, actually not easy to keep, or covered in more

investments of money and equipment for the first pet, nor the purchase of more than two specimens at first. So with these considerations, let us look at a few basic lizards.

FAMILY GEKKONIDAE—THE GECKOS

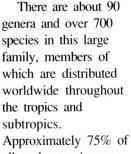

There are about 90 genera and over 700 species in this large family, members of which are distributed worldwide throughout the tropics and subtropics. Approximately 75% of all gecko species are nocturnal as evidenced by the structure of the eyes, the pupils of which contract to the narrowest of vertical slits during daytime. The pupils of the day-active (diurnal) geckos, however, are typically circular. In gecko species the body is dorsoventrally flattened or cylindrical, the scales

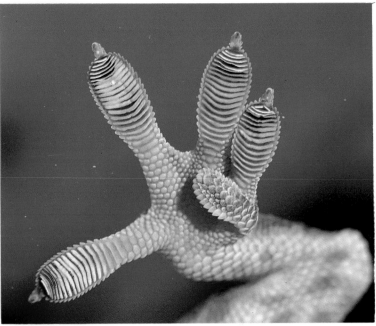

Underside of the foot of a tokay gecko showing the lamellae. Photo: K. T. Nemuras.

detail elsewhere. As captive-bred lizards become more available, the selection of basic species is sure to change to reflect this, because captive-bred (CB) lizards simply are better pets than wild-caught lizards. Before making a selection of your first lizard, discuss the available species with your dealer and if possible with another local reptile-keeper. I would not suggest heavy

are small and granular, and the skin very delicate, in some species being almost transparent. Many species have adhesive pads (technically lamellae) on the digits. Under the microscope, these lamellae can be seen to consist of rows of tiny hooks that can grip into imperfections in the most apparently smooth surfaces—even glass—, enabling the lizards to scuttle along vertical surfaces or even walk upside-down. Geckos are almost unique among lizards in being vocal. Calls differ from species to species and range from high-pitched squeaks to low quacks or barks. With the exception of the subfamily Eublepharine, the eye lacks a movable eyelid but possesses a transparent, protective brille similar to that of snakes.

Leopard Gecko
Eublepharis macularius

The leopard gecko is a large-headed, robust species with movable eyelids. At a length of a foot (30 cm), it is one of the largest common pet lizards. The skin is granular with numerous wart-like tubercles. The gray-buff ground color is strikingly marked with dark spots and blotches. It is found from Iraq to northwestern India in scrubland and semi-desert often near rocky outcrops or in gullies. Crepuscular (active at dawn and dusk), it feeds on various invertebrates and does well in captivity. It is commonly bred in captivity. Provide it with a small, dry, heated terrarium with a gravel substrate, rocks,

and one or two potted succulent plants. Daytime air temperatures of 72-82°F (22-28°C), dropping to 59°F (15°C) at night, are adequate. Keep it cooler in the winter. Feeds on a variety of invertebrates.

*Summary:*Easy to keep, relatively inexpensive, CB common.

House Gecko, Chit-Chat
Hemidactylus frenatus

Perhaps one of the most well-known geckos, the chit-chat is common in and around human

A young leopard gecko, *Eublepharis macularius*. Photo: G. Dingerkus.

habitats from hollow trees to houses, it also is common in trash dumps. A nocturnal species feeding on small invertebrates, in the tropics it is popular in houses as a "pest-controller." The chit-chat requires a tall, humid terrarium, lined with bark and furnished with one or two rocks and a couple of potted plants. Temperatures near 82°F (28°C), ...68°F (20°C) at night, are ...

...: Genus as a whole easy ...eap, often available. ...ntification difficult, some ... may have unusual ... temperature ...ts.

dwellings in many tropical parts of

Top: *Eublepharis macularius.* Bottom: *Hemidactylus turcicus.* Photos: K. T. Nemuras.

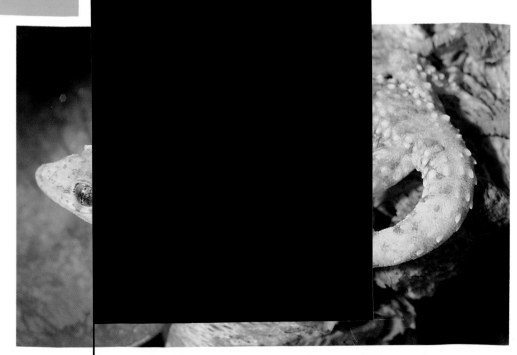

Tokay Gecko
Gekko gecko

Named for its loud, two-syllable "to-keh" call, this 12-inch (30-cm) species is one of the largest geckos. The robust body is grayish blue with numerous orange and sky-blue spots. It is a native of southern Asia from India to the Malayan Archipelago. A forest dweller, it lives in hollow limbs, behind bark, etc., and often is found in and around human habitations. This popular terrarium subject requires a tall, tropical, fairly humid terrarium with climbing branches and potted plants (*Ficus* species are ideal). Daytime temperatures may reach 86°F (30°C), reduced to 68°F (20°C) at night. It feeds on a variety of invertebrates and will take pink mice—tokays are notoriously voracious feeders.

Summary: Hardy, voracious eaters, easy to keep but may bite. Inexpensive and a lifetime pet. Noisy at times.

Kuhl's Flying Gecko
Ptychozoon kuhli

This "flying gecko" is remarkable in having webbed feet and a flap of skin along each side of the body that enable the lizard to "glide" from branch to branch. The color is brownish gray with darker mottling and incomplete bands. At 6 inches (15 cm) it is a good size for the terrarium, and certainly its bizarre appearance and behavior draw attention. A native of southeastern Asia and the adjacent island, it feeds on a variety of insects and does well at about 75-86°F (24-30°C) daytime, 68°F (20°C) nighttime temperature. A tall terrarium with many branches is of course necessary, but the humidity surprisingly should be rather low. *P. lionotum* also is available. Both species are relatively uncommon, but more and more are being bred in captivity.

Summary: Bizarre conversation piece, not too difficult, CB available, moderately inexpensive.

FAMILY IGUANIDAE—THE IGUANAS

Containing about 60 genera and over 700 species, the Iguanidae in the broad sense is one of the largest lizard families. (Recently many herpetologists have suggested that the family really contains at least eight groups of not closely related lizards that would best be recognized as distinct families. We'll stick to the more inclusive family for the time being.) Most species are American, the family ranging from southern Canada almost to the tip of South America; a few species occur on some Pacific islands (Fiji and Tonga) and Madagascar. The genera show a remarkable diversity in form, size, and habit. There is even a marine genus (*Amblyrhynchus*) on the Galapagos Islands that feeds largely on seaweed.

American Anole
Anolis carolinensis

This slender 6-8-inch (15-20-cm) lizard with a pointed snout and narrow head probably is the best known pet lizard in North America. The basic body color is green, gray, or brown, changeable to some extent depending on the reptile's mood and health. The male, which grows somewhat larger than the female, possesses an erectile bright pink to red dewlap that is displayed during territorial or sexual activity. Like many other anoles and smaller iguanids, this anole possesses adhesive lamellae under the toes and fingers and climbs very well even on seemingly smooth surfaces. A resident of the southern USA, it is found in trees and shrubs, on fences, and often in and around houses. It prefers somewhat dry areas but still needs a good humidity in its terrarium, including a daily spraying with lukewarm water. A very active diurnal, sun-loving lizard, this popular terrarium subject requires a tall terrarium with climbing branches and plants. Provide an air temperature between 75 and 85°F (24-30°C) with warmer basking areas. Reduce the temperature to around 68°F (20°C) at night. A winter rest at 57-65°F (14-18°C) is

A flying gecko, *Ptychozoon*. Notice the extensively webbed feet, which act as brakes when gliding. Photo: K. T. Nemuras.

Emerald Swift
Sceloporus malachiticus

There are dozens of spiny-scaled iguanids that are called swifts or fence lizards. They range from Canada to southern South America and the Caribbean and include such genera as *Sceloporus* (North and Central America), *Leiocephalus* (the curly-tails of the Caribbean), and *Liolaemus* (the snow swifts of southern South America). One of the most commonly available species is the emerald swift of Mexico and northern Central America, an 8-inch (20-cm) spiny often bright green lizard with large patches of turquoise on the belly and throat of the male.

Kept at 72-95°F (22-35°C) during the day and 59-72°F (15-22°C) at night in a dry terrarium with plenty of basking areas and lots of live

Top: A knight anole, *Anolis equestris*. Photo: I. Francais. Bottom: The emerald swift, *Sceloporus malachiticus*. Photo: G. Dingerkus.

recommended. Feed on a variety of small invertebrates. The foliage should be sprayed daily to provide drinking water droplets.

Summary: Wild-caught specimens often severely stressed, short-lived. May have unusual humidity requirements (depending on origin) and often hard to start feeding. Can recommend CB only.

The green anole, *Anolis carolinensis*, can assume many different colors depending on temperature, mood, and background. Photo: M. Gilroy.

insects, this species will live well and bear live young. It must be able to regulate its temperature on demand, so be sure there are cool areas in the terrarium as well as hot basking rocks. Climbing branches will be appreciated.

Summary: Spiny lizards of all types usually hardy but may have unusual humidity and temperature requirements. Big desert species spectacular but need hot basking areas to feed well. *Liolaemus* come from cool high-altitude areas and may be difficult to acclimate. *Leiocephalus* often excellent, but beware of over-stressed imports.

FAMILY AGAMIDAE— THE AGAMIDS

With over 30 genera and about 300 species, the Agamidae can be considered to be the Old World equivalent of the Iguanidae. Like the latter family, agamid species occur in a wide variety of sizes, forms, and habitats. Members of the family are widespread in Asia, Africa, and Australia.

An adult Asian water dragon, *Physignathus cocincinus*.

Asian Water Dragon

Physignathus cocincinus

Though smaller than a green iguana (family Iguanidae), this species bears a superficial resemblance to the green iguana when first seen, being of similar proportions and coloration. It even has a spiny crest extending from the nape along the back and over the long, tapering tail. A green iguana, however, has a very large round scale at the back base of the lower

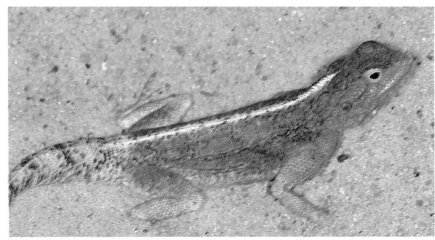

Agama atra, one of many agamid lizards that sometimes become available. Photo: P. Freed.

45

jaw that immediately separates it from the water dragon. Although green iguanas are perhaps more familiar than water dragons, they are expensive and often not as hardy. Basic color of a healthy water dragon is bright green with faint brownish bands around the body and tail and tinges of blue around the throat. There are one or two other species in the genus, all of which are inhabitants of Southeast Asia. Water dragons are arboreal, tropical forest inhabitants usually found close to water, into which they will escape if pursued. They can be very nervous in disposition, so be sure the cage is kept in a low-traffic area. Diurnal. Because of their large adult size (30 inches, 75 cm), water dragons require a large, tall terrarium with stout climbing branches and a deep pool of heated water. Maintain a high humidity and temperatures in the range of 79-86°F (26-30°C), reduced slightly at night. Feed on a variety of invertebrates and small vertebrates. May take small amounts of ripe fruit. Provide regular vitamin and mineral supplements.

Summary: Large and sometimes hard to handle. Small juveniles may be delicate and imported specimens often crowded and over-stressed. Snout injuries often severe and may require treatment. Try for well-adapted half-grown specimens, which may be quite expensive.

FAMILY SCINCIDAE—THE SKINKS

With about 50 genera and over 600 species, the Scincidae is one of the larger and more complex lizard families. Occurring on six continents, most skinks are elongate and circular in cross section with an indistinct neck. Most have smooth, glossy, overlapping scales. The majority have short but robust limbs, though in some species they are reduced or partially or totally absent. Most skinks are terrestrial or burrowing, though many climb well and a few species are partially or totally arboreal. Most are insectivorous or carnivorous, but some may take vegetable material. Many species are colorful, interesting, and settle well into captivity.

Five-lined Skink
Eumeces fasciatus

This common species of eastern North America is slender, with a long, elegant tail and a small head. It reaches about 8 inches (20 cm) in length. The young start life almost black with white or yellow stripes and a bright blue tail. As they mature, the black is replaced by an iridescent reddish brown and the tail becomes duller. Adult males often have a reddish tinge to the head, especially in the breeding season. The five-lined skink is a diurnal, terrestrial species typically found in open woodland. It requires a semi-humid to humid woodland terrarium with leaf-litter substrate. It can be kept at moderate room temperatures if warmer basking areas are provided. These skinks feed well on

Top: *Eumeces fasciatus*, the five-lined skink. Photo: R. T. Zappalorti. Bottom: *Tiliqua scincoides*, the blue-tongued skink. Photo: J. Wines.

a variety of small invertebrates and adapt well to captivity. Provide a small water dish and spray the plants regularly. Although these skinks are active during the day, they are relatively secretive and require hiding places such as pieces of bark or a hide box. They commonly climb low perches.

Summary: Hardy, often feed well, easy to keep. Secretive, so often not visible. More likely to be collected or traded than found in pet shops. Similar pet shop species often have similar requirements.

Blue-tongued Skink
Tiliqua scincoides

This is a large (18 inches, 45 cm), docile species that makes an excellent pet. It has a robust and rather elongated body with a shortish tail and short, strong limbs.

The body is light brown to silvery gray in color with darker crossbands. The fleshy, notched tongue is bright blue and often visible outside the mouth. The blue-tongue is native to eastern and northern Australia and found in a range of habitats from rain forest to dry forest and open scrubland; it often is found in suburban gardens. Diurnal, hiding in hollow logs or under ground litter at night. Produces up to 25 live young. The blue-tongue and its relatives require a large terrarium with shingle substrate, some leaf litter, and grass clumps, with hollow logs or rocks for hiding and basking. A fairly warm room temperature is sufficient, as long as a warmer (95°F, 35°C) basking area is provided. Reduce the surrounding temperature to around 68°F (20°C) at night. Medium humidity is sufficient, but provide a large, heated water bath. Because of their large size, blue-tongues can feed on a variety of invertebrates (especially snails and earthworms), pink mice, soft fruit, lean raw meat, and high quality dog or cat food.

Summary: One of the very best pet lizards but extremely expensive.

The cadillac of lizards. CB easily available.

Solomons Giant Skink
Corucia zebrata

This is one of the more unusual skinks in that it is totally arboreal and has a prehensile tail. Once rare and virtually never seen, it recently has been bred in captivity on a

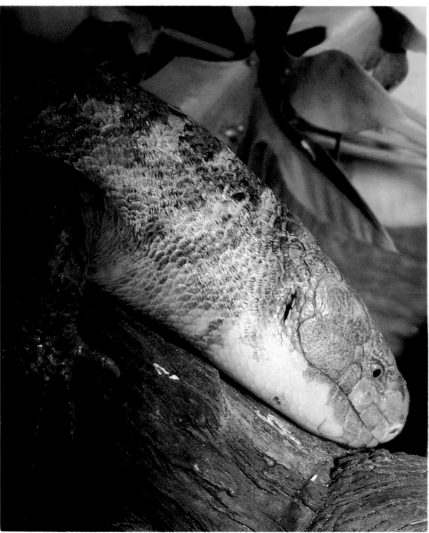

Corucia zebrata, the Solomons giant skink, recently has become a familiar but still very expensive pet lizard. Photo: R. G. Sprackland.

moderate scale and prices have come down, making it more readily available to the home enthusiast. The head is short and broad. The robust body (24 inches, 60 cm) is light olive-green with faint brown bands. Native to the Solomon Islands, it is arboreal and crepuscular to nocturnal. During the day it rests head-downward in thick vegetation or in tree hollows. To be most at home, the giant skink requires a large tropical rainforest terrarium with adequate climbing branches. Daytime temperatures may be allowed to reach 86°F (30°C), reduced to around 72°F (22°C) at night. They feed on a variety of chopped fruits and vegetables, supplemented with a little chopped boiled egg or lean raw meat. Provide a regular vitamin and mineral supplement. This species gives live-birth to one large young,

making it relatively easy to breed in captivity.

Summary: Again, one of better pet lizards but extremely expensive. CB available. Relatively new to the hobby but seems long-lived if properly care for. Large size may be a problem.

FAMILY CORDYLIDAE— SUNGAZERS AND PLATED LIZARDS

Divided into two subfamilies, the Cordylinae (sungazers or girdled lizards) and the Gerrhosaurinae (plated lizards), the family comprises some 10 genera and 40 species limited to Africa south of the Sahara and the island of Madagascar. The Cordylinae are typically spiny, with girdles of enlarged scales around the body and tail, while the Gerrhosaurinae generally are flattened with whorls of spiny scales around the tail. In most species the limbs are well developed.

Giant Sungazer
Cordylus giganteus

A fairly large (14 inches, 35 cm), sturdily built species with spiny scales all over the back and tail, this is the largest cordylid. The head is broad and triangular, with large spines at the rear of the skull. The back is mainly dark brown with darker blotches, the undersides grayish white with black speckling. A diurnal, sun-loving species of southern Africa, it lives in dry, rocky areas. Like other sungazers, it requires a large, dry

terrarium with a gravel substrate and piles of rocks. Local basking

Top: *Cordylus cataphractus*, a sungazer, coiled in defense. Photo: B. Baur. Bottom: *Dasia smaragdinum*, the green tree skink, makes a good pet. Photo: K. H. Switak.

temperatures can reach 112°F (45°C) if cooler retreats are available. Reduce the air temperature at night to about 68°F (20°C). Sungazers feed on a variety of invertebrates, raw egg, minced lean meat, etc. Provide a shallow water dish.

Summary: Readily available (many species) and moderately inexpensive. Heat and low humidity requirements may be a problem in some areas. Don't always feed well.

Sudan Plated Lizard
Gerrhosaurus major

This 16-inch (40-cm) lizard has a robust body and short but powerful limbs. The tail is long and tapering. The squarish scales are arranged in rings around the body, and there is a prominent lateral fold in the skin of the sides. The color is a uniform tan above and yellowish below. A species of eastern and southeastern Africa, it is diurnal and lives in dry, sparsely vegetated, rocky areas. Captives require a large semi-desert terrarium with a gravel substrate and a few large rocks. Daytime temperatures can reach around 86°F (30°C), with much warmer basking areas. Reduce the air temperature to around 68°F (20°C) at night. Plated lizards feed on a variety of invertebrates; some will learn to take minced lean meat, dog or cat food, and even soft, ripe fruit. Provide a shallow water bath.

Summary: Not always available

The golden plated lizard, *Gerrhosaurus auritus*, one of several similar species of the genus. Photo: J. Visser.

and may be over-stressed when found. Many people have problems with this species.

FAMILY LACERTIDAE— "TYPICAL" OLD WORLD LIZARDS

Containing some 200 species in about 22 genera, the Lacertidae is widely distributed through much of Europe, Africa, and Asia. All are similar in having a "typical" lizard shape, with an elongate body, well developed limbs, and a long, tapering tail. The upper body scales usually are small and granular, while the belly scales are large and plate-like. The large head-scales are fused to the skull. Most species are insectivorous, but a few will supplement their diet with small vertebrates or vegetation.

Green Lizard
Lacerta viridis

With an elegant tail twice the length of its head and body and a total length of about 16 inches (40 cm), this attractive species is bright green with a sprinkling of yellow and darker green spots. The male's throat becomes bright blue during the breeding season. Females and juveniles are a somewhat more somber olive-green, with a series of lighter and darker longitudinal stripes. A native of

The green lizard, *Lacerta viridis*. Photos: Top: B. Kahl; Bottom: H. Hansen.

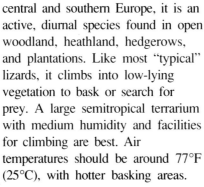

central and southern Europe, it is an active, diurnal species found in open woodland, heathland, hedgerows, and plantations. Like most "typical" lizards, it climbs into low-lying vegetation to bask or search for prey. A large semitropical terrarium with medium humidity and facilities for climbing are best. Air temperatures should be around 77°F (25°C), with hotter basking areas.

Spain, southern France, and adjacent Italy and N.W. Africa requires similar care.

Summary: Not easily available on the American market and considered delicate by many keepers. European keepers have fewer troubles with it.

Wall Lizard
Podarcis muralis

This typical lacertid (7 inches, 18

The ruins lizard, *Podarcis sicula*. Photo: B. Kahl.

Reduce the temperature to about 68°F (20°C) at night. A winter rest period of 8-10 weeks at 46-54°F (8-12°C) is recommended. Feed on a variety of invertebrates, minced lean meat, dog or cat food, and perhaps a little soft, ripe fruit. Provide a regular vitamin and mineral supplementation and a large water dish. The larger (24 inches, 60 cm) eyed lizard (*Lacerta lepida*) of

cm) comes in many subspecies and color varieties ranging through various shades of browns and greens and even black, with varying degrees of speckling and striping. A native of central and southern Europe, it is an active diurnal species, the lizard commonly seen on walls, rocky slopes, ruins, etc., in many parts of Europe. Like its relatives, it requires a rather large well-ventilated semi-humid terrarium with piles of rocks on which it can climb. The air temperature should be above 77°F (25°C) during the day, 95°F (35°C) over a basking rock, reduced to around 65°F (18°C) at night. A period of winter hibernation is

Europe. CB not readily available currently. Often considered delicate.

FAMILY TEIIDAE—TEGUS AND WHIPTAILS

With about 200 species and some 40 genera, the family Teiidae is the New World equivalent of the

Ameiva ameiva, the jungle runner. Photo: P. Freed.

recommended. Provide shallow a water bath and feed on a variety of small invertebrates. The closely related ruins lizard (*P. sicula*) of Italy and Yugoslavia requires similar care.

Summary: Like other lacertids, not that common on the American market and more likely to be seen in

lacertids, to which they bear many similarities. Distributed from northern USA through Central America to Argentina and Chile, most are typically "lizard-shaped," being slender, agile, and strong-limbed. A few, however, are almost limbless and burrowing. The body scales are granular, but those on the belly are larger and plate-like. The tail is long and elegant.

Jungle Runner
Ameiva ameiva

This 20-inch (50-cm) streamlined lizard has a robust body and longish, powerful limbs. The head is narrow with a pointed snout, and the tail is long and finely tapering. The color is extremely variable but usually shows green on the forequarters, running into brown at the rear. The jungle runner is widely distributed from southern Central America to northern South America; it also is introduced into Florida. An extremely active, diurnal species with a very "nervous" disposition, it is mainly terrestrial and excavates burrows into which it retires at night or when danger looms. Found mainly in open woodland, jungle clearings, and scrubby areas, the giant ameiva requires a relatively large terrarium with artificial burrows (such as PVC pipes or ceramic tubes), a gravel substrate, and a few prostrate plants. There should be a medium to high humidity, with air temperatures around 82°F (28°C), cooler at night. Provide the lizard with basking areas as warm as 98°F (37°C). An adult giant ameiva is an aggressive carnivore on small vertebrates and larger insects and other invertebrates. Acclimated specimens may take soft fruit, and all should be given a regular vitamin and mineral supplement. Provide a large water container.

Summary: Large size and activity may present problems. May be aggressive. Imports may be stressed. The smaller and very similar rainbow runner (*Cnemidophorus lemniscatus*) may do better but can have unusual humidity and temperature requirements. Teiids are usually considered marginally acceptable pets.

Common Tegu
Tupinambis teguixin

Tegus are probably the largest lizards a beginner is likely to successfully keep. At as much as 48 inches (120 cm), they are much heavier-bodied than longer iguanas and most monitors and much more affordable as a general rule. Basically brownish with some golden speckling, they are native to much of South America and are found in a variety of habitats from tropical rain forest to fairly arid scrubland. Terrestrial and diurnal, tegus construct burrows into which they retire at night, so sturdy hide boxes are necessary. A tegu is a powerful, active lizard with large claws and a painful tail lash, so larger specimens must be handled with care. Although the usual baby tegu will fit in a normal terrarium, remember that it will grow rapidly with good care and the adult will require a very large, secure terrarium with a large water bath. A heavy gravel substrate and a few hollow logs or artificial rocks, plus a sturdy hide box, complete the accommodations. Provide medium

stressed and die in a short while. Some specimens difficult to start feeding. Spectacular but many problems.

FAMILY ANGUIDAE—GLASS AND ALLIGATOR LIZARDS

With about 60 species in 8 genera, anguid species are found in North and South America, Europe, and Asia. All have a moderately to greatly elongated body covered in overlapping scales supported by bony cores called osteoderms. The limbs may be normal (alligator lizards), much reduced, or altogether absent (glass lizards and slow worms). The relatively long tail can be easily shed as a defense measure. Usually there is a deep scale-covered groove along the lower side that allows the abdomen to expand when the female is carrying eggs or young.

Scheltopusik
Ophisaurus apodus

The scheltopusik or Eurasian glass lizard is a large (44 inches, 110 cm) limbless lizard that is serpentine in form. The eyes are well developed, with movable lids, and the ear openings are prominent—features that help distinguish glass lizards from snakes. A prominent lateral fold runs back along the lower side from just behind the neck, ending in a tiny vestigial rear limb near the vent. The squarish scales are arranged in rings around the body. The basic color is tan to bronze-brown, yellowish beneath.

to high humidity and a daytime temperature around 90°F (32°C), reduced to not less than 72°F (22°C) at night. A good warm basking area also must be provided. Tegus feed on large invertebrates (snails especially), mice, chicks, minced lean meat, and raw eggs, all with additional vitamin and mineral supplements.

Summary: Big, aggressive lizards probably should not be chosen by beginners. Many imported specimens, especially young, are

The scheltopusik is widely distributed from eastern Europe into Asia Minor and inhabits open woodland and scrubby and rocky areas. It hides in stone walls, under rocks, and in burrows in loose soil. Oviparous, the female coils round the incubating eggs in a dark hollow. Captives need a large terrarium with a substrate of coarse sand and leaf-litter. Provide flat stones and a hollow log for hiding and basking. Daytime air and substrate temperatures can hover around 82°F (28°C), reduced to 68°F (20°C) at night. A short winter rest period at reduced temperatures (50-54°F, 10-12°C) is recommended. Provide a shallow drinking vessel. In nature scheltopusiks feed largely on garden snails, but in captivity they are voracious eaters and will accept most large invertebrates, pink mice, snails, lean meat, and similar items, including raw eggs, all with the usual vitamin and mineral supplements added. The four species of similar but generally smaller glass lizards that inhabit eastern United States require similar husbandry.

Summary: Europeans like this species and it sometimes is available in America. Not very active although may be quite large. Adaptable and long-lived. Adult imports should be checked for damage and temperament. Can have a very bad bite. American species

The eastern glass lizard, *Ophisaurus ventralis,* of the United States. Photo: R. D. Bartlett.

considered delicate, seldom successfully kept, hard to feed and secretive.

Southern Alligator Lizard
Gerrhonotus multicarinatus

Alligator lizards are moderate-size (12 inches, 30 cm) rather slender lizards with a long tails and well-developed limbs. There is a lateral fold of skin between the fore and rear limbs. The color is variable but is usually an attractive pattern of dark brown and yellow arranged in bars, bands, and blotches. This species is found in western North America from southern Washington to Baja California in open woodlands, grasslands, and relatively damp areas. Primarily diurnal, it climbs into shrubs in search of prey, so provide it with a large, tall, planted terrarium with climbing facilities. Maintain a daytime air temperature around 77°F (25°C), with warmer basking sites, and reduce the temperature at night to 65-68°F (18-20°C). A short winter rest period at a reduced temperature is recommended. Feed this alligator lizard on a variety of small invertebrates dusted with a vitamin and mineral supplement. Provide a small drinking vessel and spray the terrarium plants two or three times per week.

Summary: Alligator lizards in general are good pets and fairly inexpensive. May have unusual humidity requirements, and some are from cool mountains, so species identification essential. Often voracious eaters. Since some give live birth, are often CB.

FAMILY VARANIDAE— MONITOR LIZARDS

This small family contains a single genus confined to the Old World tropics, including Australia. The Komodo dragon, *Varanus komodoensis*, which reaches a length of over 10 feet (3 m) and is a heavy-

A savannah monitor (bottom) compared to a common tegu. Photo: I. Francais.

bodied species, is the largest living lizard species. Other species range in size from under 16 inches (40 cm) to almost 10 feet (3 m), though the larger species tend to be very slender in build. All have well-developed limbs and a powerful, whip-like tail used in defense. The head usually is long, with a pointed snout, large teeth, and powerful jaws. All are carnivorous, feeding on a range of animals and carrion. Due to their large size and aggressive disposition, most monitor species are not recommended as pets for beginners.

Savannah Monitor
Varanus exanthematicus

Currently the savannah monitor is the most easily available monitor and perhaps the only one a beginner should even consider. At about 6 feet in adult length (200 cm) it is a handful, requiring large quarters, heavy feeding, and careful handling, but it is moderately adaptable to handling. It requires a very large terrarium, preferably with a heated, drainable concrete pool. Maintain temperature around 79-86°F (26-30°C) day and night throughout the year. A warm basking area is of course required. Like most other monitors, it feeds on mice, rats, chicks, eggs, raw meat, and dog or cat food. With constant attention, specimens reared from hatchlings will become tame and trusting, though large wild-caught specimens rarely lose their natural aggressiveness.

Summary: Although many specialists like monitors, they are

Varanus acanthurus, one of the small Australian monitors. Photo: W. B. Allen, Jr.

Top: A juvenile *Amphibolurus barbatus*, the Australian bearded dragon, captive-bred. Photo: W. B. Allen, Jr. Bottom: *Tiliqua branchialis*, a rarely seen blue-tongued skink. Photo: K. H. Switak.

problem animals and cannot be recommended for beginners. Except for dwarf species (virtually never available), pet shop juveniles become monsters with large terrarium requirements and often horrible temperaments. A large monitor, even the relatively placid savannah, can hurt you. Imports often are severely stressed and die shortly after arrival. CB only, and only if you cannot do without one.

INDEX